Contents

00. Prelude - The Essence of Now

00. Intermission - A Painter's Eye

Prelude - The Essence of Now

In the heat of the moment, the place to be
Lessons along the way as I continue to fall forward
That time is now, a graceful realization
Collection of experiences guide as a teacher of life
Whats understood may only be understood
What point in explaining what your heart desires
Motion of moving onward lead to a vast destination of endless possibilities

How grateful I am to have memories consisting of great times and great
friends. Thank you.

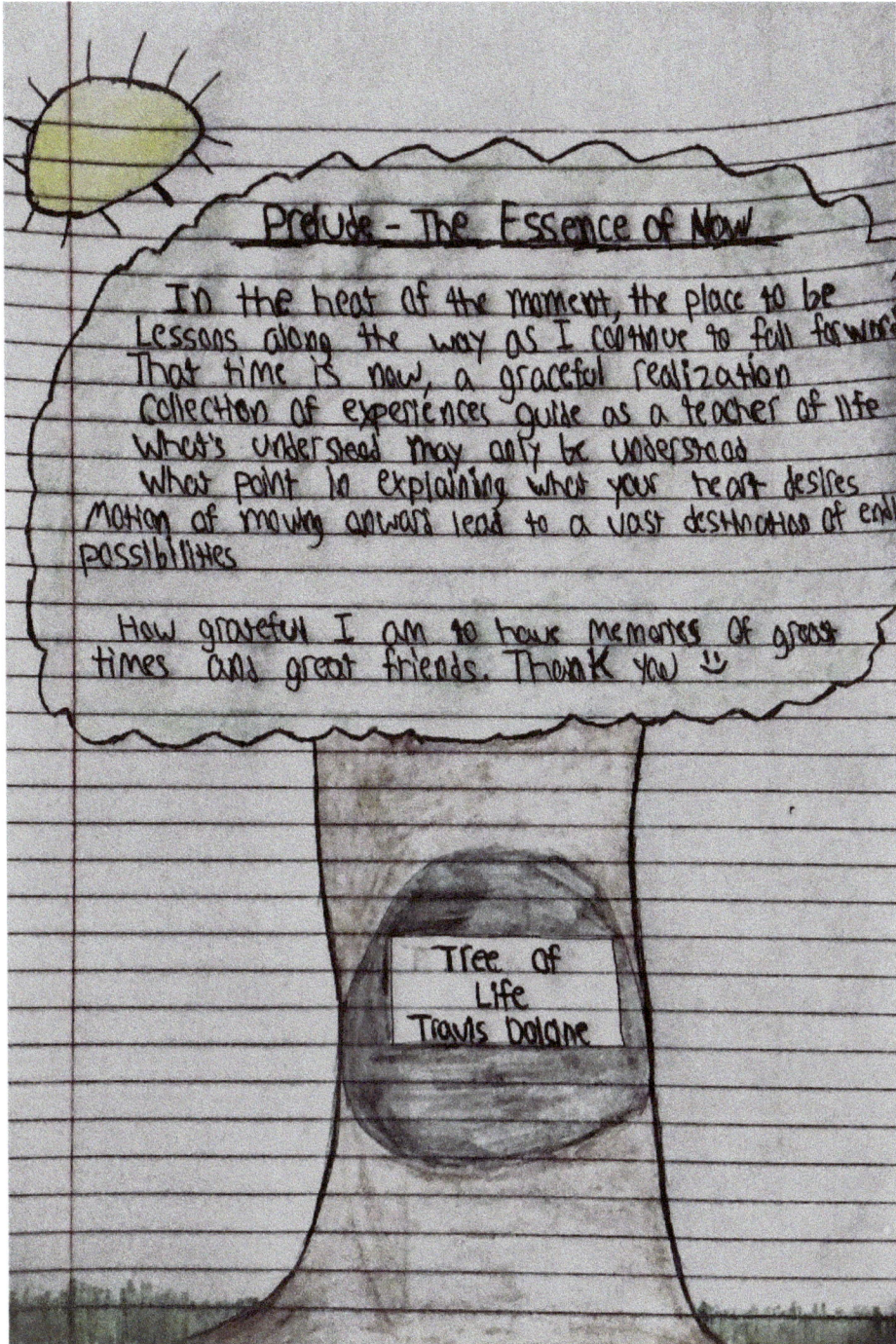

Prelude - The Essence of Now

In the heat of the moment, the place to be
Lessons along the way as I continue to fall forward
That time is now, a graceful realization
Collection of experiences guide as a teacher of life
What's understood may only be understood
What point in explaining what your heart desires
Motion of moving onward lead to a vast destination of endless possibilities

How grateful I am to have memories of great times and great friends. Thank you :)

Tree of
Life
Travis Dolane

In this Moment (Letter 2 Future)

In this moment I breathe
In this moment I feel a breeze

I believe in myself and what can be achieved
Faith Nd Finesse is already done
Just be with intent and you'll become

For these moments I am relieved

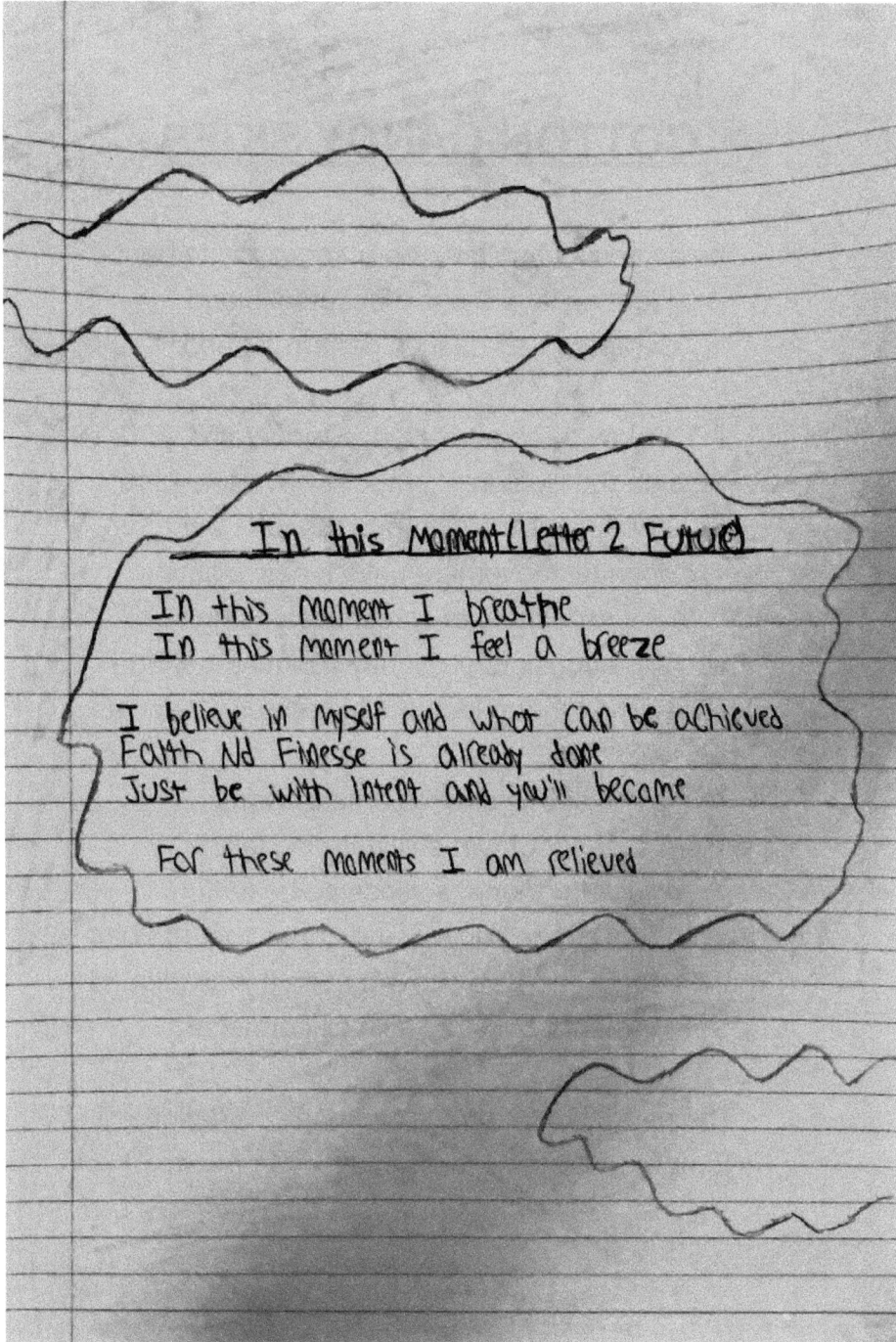

In this Moment (Letter 2 Future)

In this moment I breathe
In this moment I feel a breeze

I believe in myself and what can be achieved
Faith Nd Finesse is already done
Just be with Intent and you'll become

For these moments I am relieved

COTTON CANDY SKIES

The osmosis of colors, the burst of excitement
Floating layers pile a beautiful blend
Separated by dashes pattern a trend

Below the blends lay the mountains
Plays on the illusion of smooth wave-like form
Trees in the near shroud the full view
Continual movement unlock new sights
As if a slideshow of screens was running
Each slide consists of slightly a different shade
Depending on the reflections of natures obstacles

The subtle strokes create a fade
A fade far off yet still warming inside
A feeling of one, a sense so beautiful
A mixture so fine as the sun's orange glare met the blue sky
You'd want to take a piece but everythings aligned
Moments of clarity as it all connects

The perfection of timing an image so defined
Temporary to the eye, Everlasting in the mind

Cotton Candy Skies

The osmosis of colors, the burst of excitement
Floating layers pile a beautiful blend
Separated by dashes pattern a trend

Below the blends lay the mountains
Plays on the illusion of smooth wave-like form
Trees in the near shroud the full view
Continual movement unlocking new sights
As if a slideshow of screens was running
Each slide consists of slightly a different shade
Depending on the reflections of natures obstacles

The subtle strokes create a fade
A fade far off yet still warming inside
A feeling of one, a sense so beautiful
A mixture so fine as the sun's orange glare met the blue sky
You'd want to take a piece but everythings aligned
Moments of clarity as it all compacts

The perfection of timing so defined
Temporary to the eye, Everlasting in the mind

What's True

You can finesse me; but you can't finesse what's for me

Floating to the surface, gazing into the blues
Desperately unfolding when the times seemed true
Gasping for air when the opportunity arises
Overcoming the waves as lifes full of surprises
Flow, as they say, a story to observe
Power to you, a feeling so deserved

You can finesse me; but you can't finesse what's for me

What's True

You can finesse me; but you can't finesse wheus for me

Floating to the surface gazing into the blues
Desperately unfolding when the times seemed true
Gasping for air when the opportunity arises
Overcoming the waves as lifes full of surprises
Flow, as they say, a story to observe
Power to you, a feeling so deserved

You can finesse me; but you can't finesse wheus for me

Meditate N' Relate

In you, not on you

Beyond the dark, there's a light
A world so true, free from freight   (breathe)

In you, not on you

Time in time, you realize alright
Graciously growing reaching new heights   (breathe)

In you, not on you

A passion burning, feelings ignite
Incite these lines after tonite   (breathe)

In you, not on you

Meditate N' Relate

In you, not on you

Beyond the dark, there's a light
A world so true, free from freight (— (breathe)

In you, not on you

Time in time, you realize alright
Graciously growing reaching new heights ((breathe)

In you, not on you

A passion burning, feelings ignite
Incite these lines after tonite ((breathe)

In you, not on you

<u>Still Water</u>

As I stand between two bodies of water
Reflection from the surfacetop wasn't the only takeaway

To my left still water with tiny ripples created by gust of wind
Hitting the land in unison as if it were man-made
Slowly changing direction as the wind takes its course
A more calming feel and simple pattern to make note of

To my right still water with chaotic motion
Hitting different parts of the shore at different times and speed
Waves created that seem to be rocking back and forth violently
A more distressed feel and less effective unison pattern

To my left was a pond which seemed like effortless flow
The amazement of nature taking its own course

Whereas to my right was more of open body of water
The wind clashing against each other in multiple directions
Seemed like a forced flow with no true sense of direction

Still Water

As I stood between two bodies of water
Reflection from the surfacetop wasn't the only takeaway

To my left still water with tiny ripples created by gust of wind
Hitting the land in unison as if it were man-made
Slowly changing direction as the wind takes it course
A more calming feel and simple pattern to make note of

To my right still water with chaotic motion
Hitting different parts of the shore at different times and speed
waves created that seem to be rocking back and forth violently
A more distressed feel and less effective unison pattern

To my left was a pond which seemed like effortless flow
The amazement of nature taking its own course

Whereas to my right was more of open body of water
The wind clashing against each other in multiple directions
seemed like a forced flow with no true sense of direction

Dreaming Awake (Letter 2 my Love)

What I thought was only a dream slowly turned to reality
What I feared deeply inside feels safe in your hands

For your soul feels like home no need for protection
I cherished the hardships that helped with direction
No more confusion, a blissful connection
Use my words as a stepping stool to express how much I care
Lost and found, a burning passion rekindled
I had to die before I woke up, to be here in this moment

A dream of a dream that became a reality
A shared love that was once fantasized upon
Thank you for hearing my heart

Dreaming Awake (Letter 2 My Love)

What I thought was only a dream turned to reality
What I feared deeply inside feels safe in your hands

For your soul feels like home no need for protection
I cherished the hardships that helped with direction
No more confusion, a blissful connection
Use my words as a stepping stool to express how much I care
Lost and found, a burning passion rekindled
I had to die before I woke up, to be here in this moment

A dream of a dream that became reality
A shared love that was once fantasized upon
Thank you for hearing my heart

Rain Showers

Like the beat of a drum, the thrill of not knowing the end
My heart beats in similar fashion, filled with excitement
Silently listening as each drop so calming during our ascend
Effortlessly flowing w/ the wind current, a promising commitment

The transition of a heavy rain to one of lighter sound
Transformation that required deep roots in the ground
Seeming far off in distance but constantly surrounds
The moment of clarity as love can be so profound

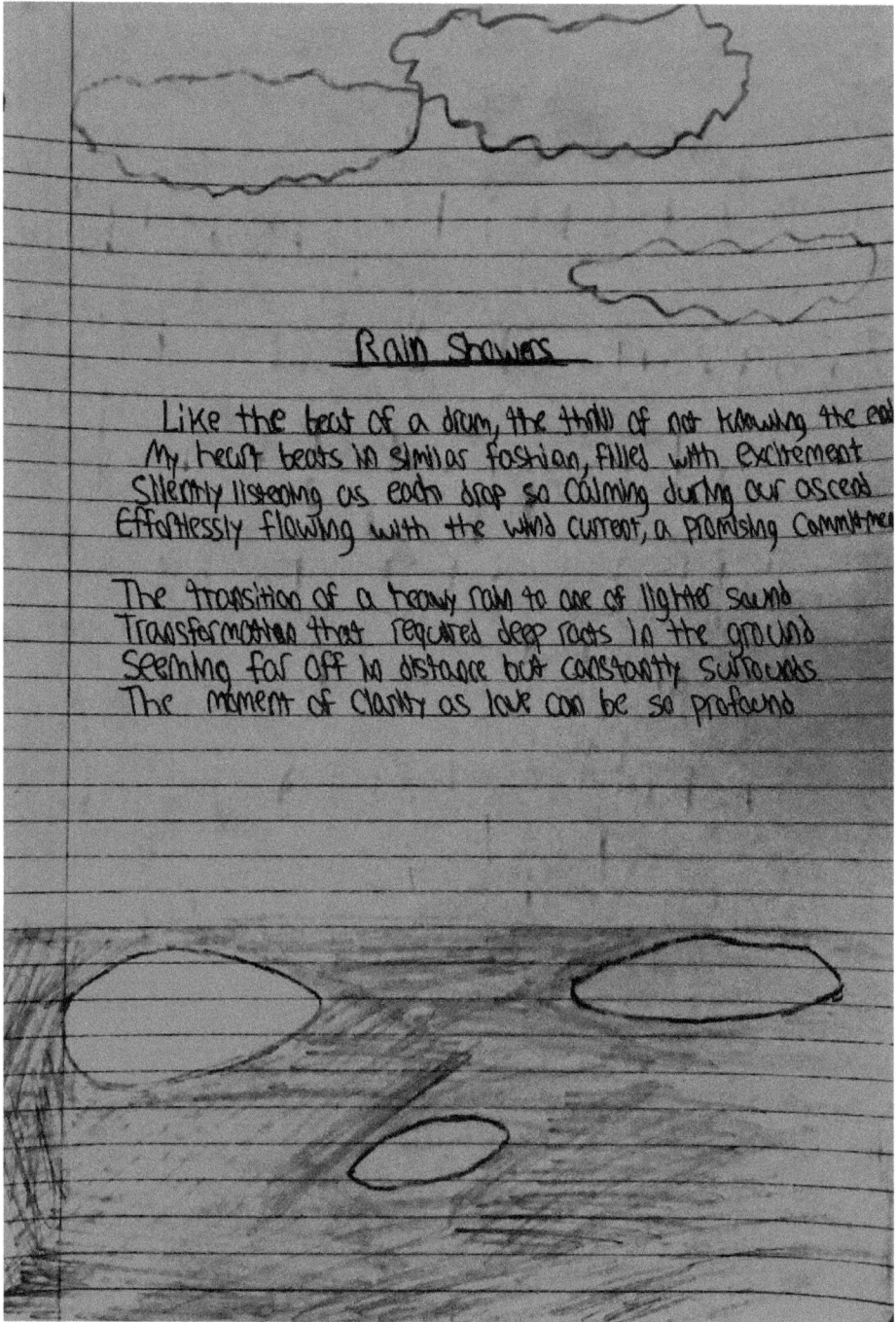

Rain Showers

Like the beat of a drum, the thrill of not knowing the end
My heart beats in similar fashion, filled with excitement
Silently listening as each drop so calming during our ascend
Effortlessly flowing with the wind current, a promising commitment

The transition of a heavy rain to one of lighter sound
Transformation that required deep roots in the ground
Seeming far off in distance but constantly surrounds
The moment of clarity as love can be so profound

<u>Afternoon Skies 7:17</u>

As the nighttime falls before me
A midnight blue hovers the last of teal orange
The glimmer of stars
The sacrifice for a dream
Growth that lies between
All in a moment
The breath… so fresh

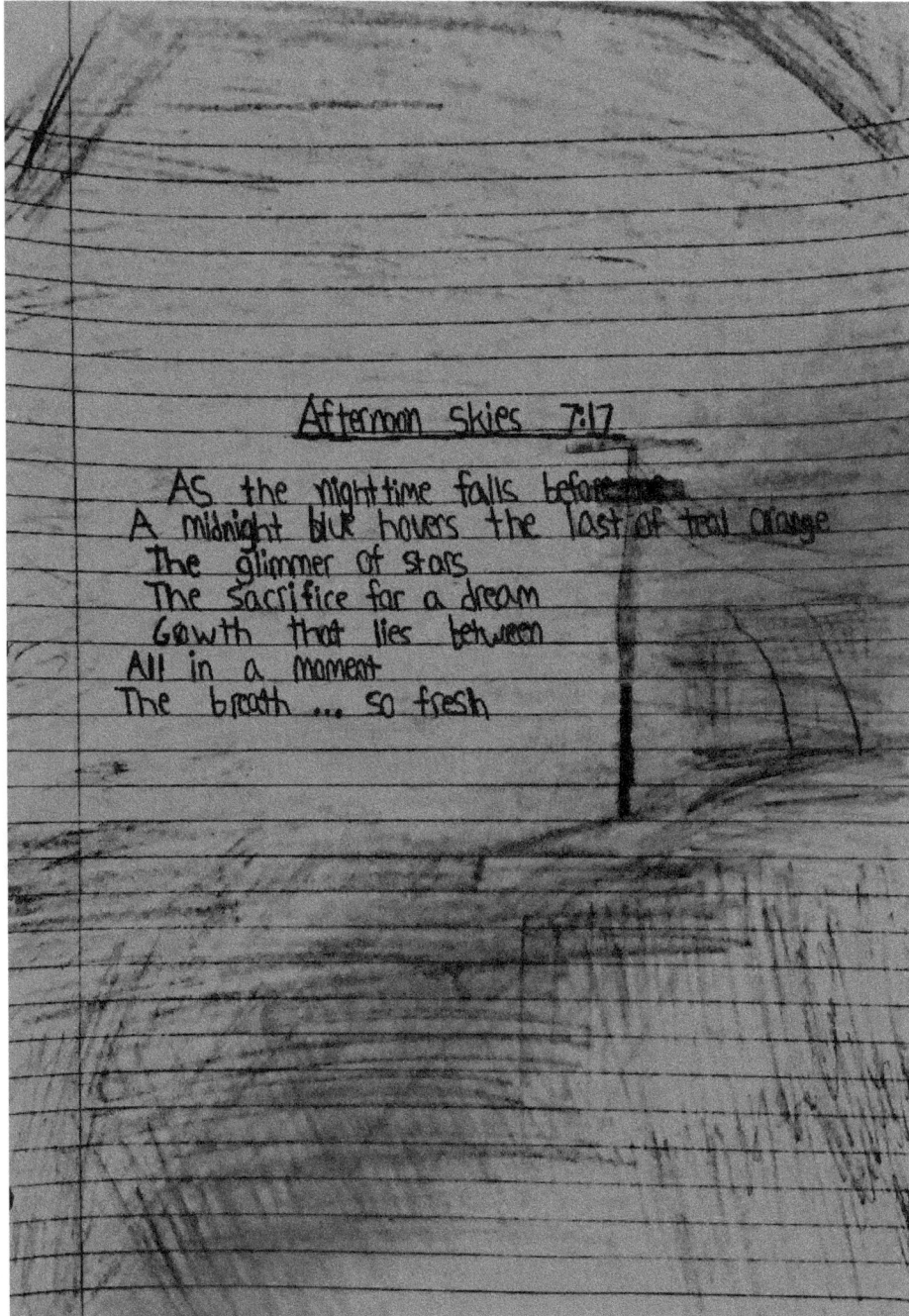

Afternoon skies 7:17

AS the nighttime falls before
A midnight blue hovers the last of teal orange
The glimmer of stars
The sacrifice for a dream
Gowth that lies between
All in a moment
The breath ... so fresh

<u>Wd View 11:41</u>

The terrace and road connects
Rush of changing perspectives
Illuminating grass makes fall
Pop like the colors
Red, Orange and Yellow
In addition an ominous misty blue covers

Wd View 11:41

The terrace and road connect
Rush of changing perspectives
Illuminating grass makes fall
Pop like the colors
Red, orange and yellow
In addition an ominous misty blue covers

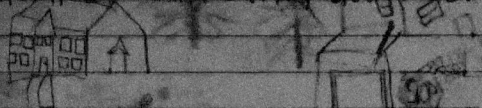

<u>Peace</u>

Deep focus in the beauty of the moment
Intensity brought silence to the external
Silence of thoughts
Indulged in the vast what seems endless waves of water
The brightness of the sun's glare instantly as it meets the horizon

To understand the glistening of life's waves
The visual of fast approaching waves crashing right before you
Was there no need for worry as it figures it self out before you
Surrender to the moments that serve as guidance
A play to observe when your courageous to dance to life's song

Peace

Deep focus in the beauty of the moment
Intensity brought silence to the external
Silence of thoughts
Indulged in the vast what seems endless waves of water
The brightness of the sun's glare instantly as it meets the horizon

To understand the glistening of life's waves
The visual of fast approaching waves crashing right before you
Was there no need for worry as it figures it self out before you
Surrender to the moments that serve as guidance
A play to observe when your courageous to dance to life's song

Intermission - A Painter's Eye

Picture perfect or perfect picture
The amazement of imagination or the fascination of timing
The gift to see, the curse of interpretation

How might one see how you see
Or rather see through the same lens
A soul yearns for creative ways to express
Passionately striving to make ways towards one's imagined success

Perception becomes reality or is reality a perception
Art inspired by life or is Life an art

Intermission - A Painter's Eye

Picture perfect or perfect picture
The amazement of imagination or the fascination of timing
The gift to see, the curse of Interpretation

How might one see how you see
or rather see through the same lens
A soul yearns for creative ways to express
Passionately striving to make ways towards ones imagined success

Perception becomes reality or is reality a perception
Art inspired by life or is life an art

CHANGES

When the leaves fall w/ the wind
Is this you letting go
Was it time for your new skin to glow
Radiant colors change w/ the season
As for your foundation, it stays the same
Resilient in love as if the wind don't mean a thing

Changes

When the leaves fall w/ the wind
Is this you letting go
Was it time for your new skin to glow
Radiant Colors change w/ the season
As for your foundation, it stays the same
Resilient in love as if the wind don't mean a thing

<u>Picture me Smiling (:</u>

Bliss what I'm feeling
Real EYE how I'm seeing
Real lies, realize truth what I'm seekin

Back to the world, like a game of connect the dots
Imagine a smile and my eyes as the flames
Connect the dots and you'd see the same

A play on words so the brain plays the game
Tell me what's broken if my smile remains unchanged

Picture Me Smiling (:

Bliss what I'm feeling
Real EYE how I'm seeing
Real lies, realize truth what I'm seekin

Back to the wand like a game of connect the dots
Imagine a smile and my eyes as the flames
connect the dots and you'd see the same

A play on words so the brain plays the game
Tell me whats broken if my smile remains unchanged

<u>Remember my Laughter</u>

A day filled with laughter brought a night full of silence

Burst of energetic screeches imployed in gratitude
Along w/ vibrantful moments determined by attitude
A splash of sporadic tears may meet the eye
Captured thru lens that magnify a great degree of aptitude
Reflect on the times as you find yourself in solitude

Peace of mind, to have a lovely time
When it's time for packing, those brief moments we share
I ask you, remember my laughter…

Remember my Laughter

A day filled with laughter brought a night full of silence

Burst of energetic screeches imployed in gratitude
Along with vibrantful moments determined by attitude
A splash of sporadic tears may meet the eye
Captured thru lens that magnify a great degree of aptitude
Reflect on the times as you find yourself in solitude

Peace of mind, to have a lovely time
When it's time for packing, those brief moments we store
I ask you remember my laughter...

<u>In the Midst of it All</u>

Turmoil on the outside
Observant of the inside
A game that unravels, one that provides
Life's clues, serve as guides
To die before you have died
No said losses if the lesson is applied

In the Midst of it All

Turmoil on the outside
Observant of the inside
A game that unravels, one that provides
Lifes clues, serve as guides
To die before you have died
No said losses if the lesson is applied

In Still, I Stand

Outside pressure merely an illusion
Negative thoughts bring quite confusion
Mind of his own, a mighty solution
Dawn find the day profound in exclusion

Solitude holds magnitude
Along with great gratitude
Misunderstood with a plan
In still, I stand

In Still, I stand

Outside pressure merely an illusion
Negative thoughts bring quite confusion
Mind of his own, a mighty solution
Dawn find the day profound in exclusion

Solitude holds magnitude
Along with great gratitude
Misunderstood with a plan
In Still, I stand

Path Left Untraveled

Into the unknown with a brave start
The abundance of trees shield the wildlife terrain
Prioritizing your path; make space for ways to part
Trails unmarked enduring the confusion and pain
Where the traveler ends up to the desire of their heart

Path Left Untraveled

Into the Unknown with a brave Start
The abundance of trees shield the wildlife terrain
Prioritizing your path; make space for ways to part
Trails unmarked enduring the confusion and pain
Where the traveler ends up to the desire of their heart

<u>See Me 4 Me</u>

Letting go of the image I thought was needed
Death of the mind's protective walls succeed
To see me past the hurt, the true me
Reconciled with the innocence that always been me
To see the world as you are
Breaking threshold limits into the unknown
Process of vulnerability dissociation of the ego
To live a life where other beings see me 4 me

See Me 4 Me

Letting go of the image I thought was needed
Death of the mind's protective walls succeed
To see me past the hurt, the true me
Reconciled with the innocence that always been me
To see the world as you are
Breaking threshold limits into the unknown
Process of vulnerability dissociation of the ego
To live a life where other beings see me 4 me

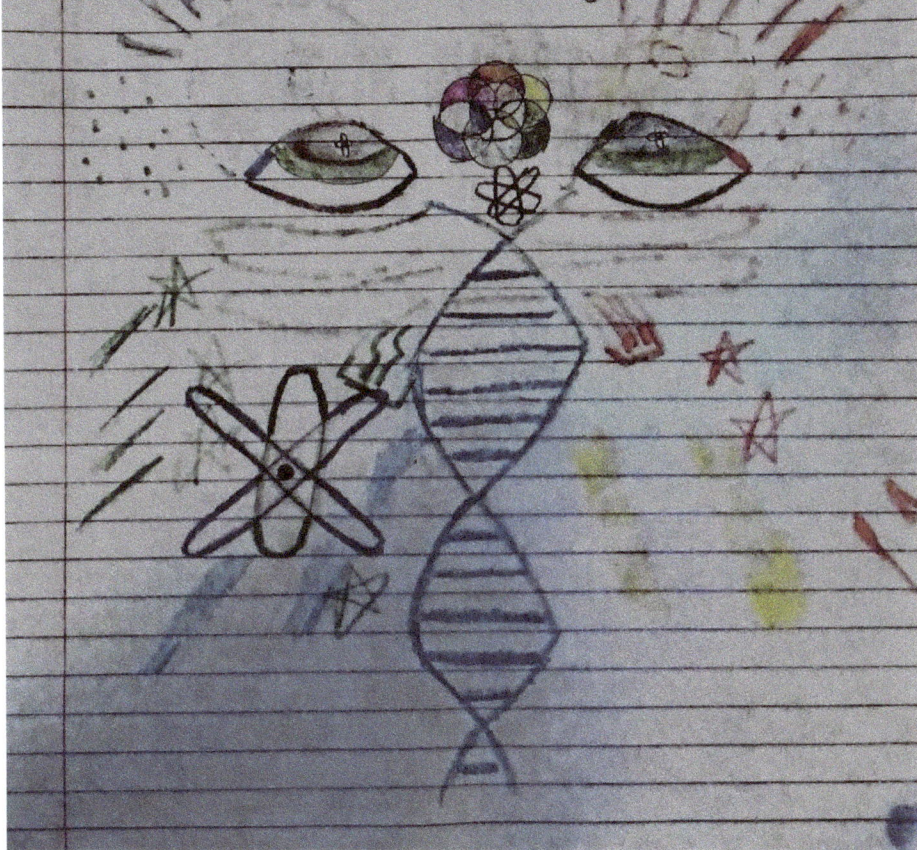

The Silent Battle

The difference between 6ix and n9ne
Only a patient heart will understand
Answers lie within the silence
There may not be anything to explain
My mind runs wild with trying to solve relations
But the answers will always lie within the silence
Become slave to words or embrace the power of limitless

Problems dissolve if fed no context
Beware of the silent battle within

The Silent Battle

The difference between 6ix and nine
Only a patient heart will understand
Answers lie within the silence
There may not be anything to explain
My mind runs wild trying to solve relations
But the answers will always lie within the silence
Become a slave to words or embrace the power of limitle

Problems dissolve if fed no context
Beware of the silent battle within

<u>Free Spirit</u>

Adolescence in essence
Behind the worry and fear

Purpose, oh purpose
A depth of living

Imagination run wild
Full of intent

Broken shackles
Rid of constraint

Connected as one
The fun has begun

Free Spirit

Adolescence in essence
Behind the worry and fear

Purpose, oh purpose
A depth of living

Imagination run wild
Full of intent

Broken shackles
Rid of constraint

Connected as one
The fun has begun

Rose in the Wind

Perseverance what comes to mind
Withstanding the outside pressure as the visual
Carried along by the wind
Soaring through experiences of life

Keeping form yet growing
Blooming yet seeded
Withering yet transforming
Alone yet divinely guided

Leaving a trail of petals to be unraveled
A wayward soul perhaps in search of the beauty within
An imperfect rose perhaps brushing along the unknown

Rose in the Wind

Perseverance What comes to mind
Withstanding the outside pressure as the visual
Carried along by the wind
Soaring through experiences of life

Keeping form yet growing
Blooming yet seeded
Withering yet transforming
Alone yet divinely guided

Leaving a trail of petals to be unraveled
A wayward soul perhaps in search of beauty within
An imperfect rose perhaps brushing along the unknown

<u>Autumn Leaves</u>

By the look of the eyes, the rain has passed
Embracing the transition, the change of colors
The combination of red, yellow and orange
Acceptance of it all plays a beautiful setting
The suns ray lighting forward
Highlighting the fall, recognizing a reality

year 24

The final act? The true essence of me
Sum of it all, no label to me
Where fear ridden desires to be

<u>Magical Morning Moon</u>

Meaningful dream with a kiss from my love
Moment that translated a feeling so bliss
Dream of a dream or am I finally awake?

Into an unknown seeming like a mixture of day n' night
Bright blue sky with the presence of a mystical full moon
Mark of a completed lunar phase cycle?

Mastering the art of being
Marvelous time of heightened possibilities
Miracles await with no expectations

Mirrored reflection alters a reality

Magical Morning Moon

Meaningful dream w/ a kiss from my love
Moment that translated a feeling so bliss
Dream of a dream or am I finally awake?

Into an unknown seeming like a mixture of day n night
Bright blue sky w/ the presence of a mystical full moon
Mark of a completed lunar phase cycle

Mastering the art of being
Marvelous time of heightend possibilites
Miracles await with no expectations

Mirrored reflection alters a reality

THE END OR IS IT ...

THE BEGINNING ?

Truth is the only safe ground to stand upon...